Getting the Appointment Handbook

STUDENT EDITION

www.theultimatetoolkit.com

Jon Spoelstra & Steve DeLay

GETTING THE APPOINTMENT HANDBOOK

The path to becoming a superstar

Jon Spoelstra & Steve DeLay
December, 2013

Getting the Appointment Handbook

Welcome. From this point forward your life will change. You'll be learning ome important skill that you will be able to use for the rest of your life: how to get an appointment with anybody.

When you learn these fundamentals in this Handbook, you can make an appointment with anybody you want.

This is an exceptionally valuable skill to possess. Less than 1% of Americans possess these skills.

It's not that dfficult to learn these skills. But, you do have to *precisely* follow the instructions. This means no ad-libbing, no individualizing, no modifying.

After you fully learn these skills, you may customize them a bit. However, in the learning process, stay the course we have set in this booklet.

Have fun. You'll enjoy the ride. You'll really enjoy the benefits.

Jon Spoelstra

Steve DeLay

HOW THIS BOOKLET WORKS

There are two sides to each page. The left side (what you're reading right now) is me talking to you. The right side (see the word 'you') is you, and what you're saying.

You don't see any words by 'you' because right now I'm doing all the talking. When you're talking, it will be the actual words that you need to use to get the appointment with a CEO. We put these words into a format we call Telechart Cards. These cards are convenient to carry around and can be spread out in front of you when you're making phone calls for appointments. You need to use these Telechart Cards *word-for-word*.

I'm here to help you. I'll comment in two places: 1) the left side of the page; and 2) **Stage direction** comments on the right side of the page.

You don't have to memorize what I say, just take it in, even if it seems unconventional. Years from now when you have a lot more experience, you'll look back at this and say, 'Wow, he was right.'

You

(Blank space on the right side means that you're silent. You're busy reading and thinking. Good.)

WHAT YOU NEED TO DO TO SUCCEED

For you to succeed as an outside ticket salesperson, there is one thing you *must* do. This *one thing* is absolutely necessary.

That one thing is: **You *MUST* make 12 sales calls per week.**

These sales calls must be made by appointments, not by just grabbing somebody in a coffee shop and giving them a spiel.

Get used to this benchmark: 12 sales calls per week made from appointments. That's the benchmark. Anything fewer than 12 sales calls per week is not acceptable.

Already I can hear some protests. What if you're a really slick salesperson, can you make only eight sales calls per week? Nope. You will fail. What about ten sales calls per week? Nope.

What if you're a salesperson that doesn't have much experience in sales? Well, if that's the case, you should try to make *more than* 12 sales calls per week. That's like taking extra batting practice to perfect your swing. If you make *at least* 12 sales calls a week, you will be very effective in closing sales. Heck, if you make 15 sales calls every week, you might become the star salesperson on the staff. However, if you make fewer than 12, you will fail miserably.

You

(Blank space on the right side means that you're silent and still reading.)

(Yep, you're still quiet and paying attention.)

(

PREDICTING SUCCESS OR FAILURE

How do we know who is going to succeed or fail? How can we *predict* success or failure? Ticket sales is a numbers game, and we've worked with hundreds of young ticket salespeople. The magic number for success is 12 sales calls per week. Fewer than that either leads to mediocrity or outright failure.

You could try to challenge this and prove us wrong. And, what if you did prove us wrong? What do you win? You 'win' the fact that you could've been really successful by making the benchmark of 12 sales calls per week.

If you think I believe that quality appointments are the bedrock of selling success then you think correctly.

HERE'S HOW TO GET THOSE APPOINTMENTS

You will need three things to be effective in getting an appointment:

1. **Who to call.** Your territory and list of prospects will be provided by your Sales Manager. You'll be calling on corporations that are non-retail, non-government, or non-profits. Your target is the Chief Executive Officer or President or top business person of the company.

(Don't worry, you'll get a chance to talk.
Just be patient right now and learn.)

2. **Number of prospects.** You'll have about 1,000 in your protected territory. Those are companies that have 10 or more employees. There are an additional 2,000 companies (non-retail, non-government, non non-profits) that you can call on that have 5-10 employees.

3. **When to call to get the appointment.** Contrary to popular opinion, *chief executive officers are accessible* to outsiders. Sure, they might be positioned in an ivory tower by the gatekeeper (executive secretary or administrative assistant), but there is a way of piercing that tower. When you do, you find an executive that is often more accessible than the rank-and-file executive. The CEO will be friendly, attentive, knows what he or she likes, *and knows which executive to send you to in order to finish off the details of the transaction.*

   If you want an appointment with the CEO, you can't get it unless you use some unusual strategy. Here's the truth about the strategy:

> The best time to reach a CEO is when the gatekeeper
> is ***not*** there.

So, when isn't the gatekeeper there? Figure that the gatekeeper works from about 8:30am to about 5:30pm, give or take a half hour each way. What window of opportunity does that leave you?

(You may be thinking: why do all of this? Why not just send an email or text for an appointment? Again, be patient, you'll find out.)

- 7:15-8:00am

- 12:15-1:00pm (yes, gatekeepers often go out for lunch)

- 5:30-6:30pm

It's not a question if these are the most efficient times to call for an appointment. It is the most efficient. The real question is actually three questions you must answer yourself:

Question #1: Do you have the drive and guts to come into the office at 7:00am, get yourself ready to make the first phone call at 7:15am?

Question #2: Do you have the drive and guts to stay late and start making appointment calls at 5:45pm?

Question #3: Will you prepare a list of 50 prospects the night *before* you call them?

If you answer *yes* to each of those questions then here's what your morning will be like.

(Getting the appointment with the right person is, by far, the toughest part of making the sale. If you can make the appointment, and you follow the explicit steps in **The Ultimate Toolkit's** *Getting the Sale*, you've got better than a 50-50 chance in making the sale.)

- You dedicate the early morning and late afternoon times for making appointments. This isn't a time to read emails. Or talk to others in the office. Or for any outside meetings. Call for appointments!

- To make 12 appointments each week, a salesperson will likely have to make 40-50 phone calls each day. These are 40-50 phone calls just to make appointments. That's Monday thru Thursday and sometimes Friday. You'll be working from a list of 50 prospects that you prepared the night before. (Don't waste time in the morning preparing your call list; do it the night before.)

- Some days you'll get seven connects from your 40 phone calls. Of those seven connects, you might get three appointments. As you get more experienced, you'll get 5-6 appointments from those seven connects.

- The total time spent to make 40-50 phone calls and get seven connects is about twenty minutes. After all, you're talking to only those prospects that answer the phone. For the non-answers, you just hang up and note the time and date that you called that prospect.

Here's what your week would look like:

ime	Mon.	Tues.	Weds.	Thurs.	Fri.	Sat.	Sun
7:15a to 8:00a	Make 40 calls for appts	Make 40 phone calls for appts	Make 40 phone calls for appts	Make 40 phone calls for appts	Make 40 calls for appts		
8:15a to Noon	On appts	On appts	On appts	On appts	On appts	Make 20 appt calls	
12:30p to 1:00p	15 Phone calls for appts	15 Phone calls for appts	15 Phone calls for appts	15 phone calls for appts	15 phone calls for appts		
1:00p to 5:00p	On appts	On appts	On appts	On appts	On appts		
5:30p to 6:30p	15 Phone calls for appts	15 Phone calls for appts	15 Phone calls for appts	15 Phone calls for appts			

WHAT TO SAY WHEN IT'S TIME TO SAY IT

Never make a cold call on the phone without: 1) knowing what you are going to say; 2) knowing what the prospect will say and; 3) knowing how you will respond to the prospect.

The best time to know what to say and how you will respond to a prospect is *long before* the phone call is made. Let me explain.

Early in my career, even before I got into professional sports, I started calling on CEOs of major companies. I was fall-down-shaking nervous in making the phone call for an appointment. I decided I needed some big-time help. I went to guys who had been my idols for several years, sales trainers like Jack Lacy, Fred Herman, Heartsell Wilson, and Red Motley and I re-read their books and re-listened to their tapes and read some of the newer guys.

I felt I needed a 'cheat sheet' when phoning for appointments. Basically these were *scripts* that I wrote out on the old key-punch cards. The cards were sturdy and would fit in my jacket pocket. On these cards were the *exact words* I was going to say in introducing myself over the phone. Also, on these cards were the *exact words* I was going to say when responding to an objection.

I practiced reading these cards aloud. Even though I knew them by heart, I would lay out the cards on my desk when making appointment calls. When the CEO actually answered the phone, my nerves were shot, but I picked up the first card and JUST READ THE CARD.

(It's getting close.)

When the CEO objected about seeing me, I JUST READ THE APPROPRIATE RESPONSE CARD. I got the appointment. Time after time.

.*JUST READ THE CARD!*

After awhile, I felt I could get an appointment with anyone. One of my buddies challenged me into making an appointment with the President of the United States. I declined the challenge. Sure, I could have made the appointment, but I didn't have anything to sell him.

In the 1990's, as president of the New Jersey Nets, I took that same concept but printed my phone scripts onto 3" x 8" cards, which I now called Telechart Cards. I worked with our outside salespeople on how to get appointments with CEOs. These salespeople were all young and inexperienced. To a person, they were clearly intimidated on phoning a CEO. However, once they were trained on the Telechart Cards, and made it part of their life, it worked like magic in a market where no CEO wanted to see somebody from the then-hapless Nets.

I'll take you step-by-step through all the Telechart Cards and why we say what we say to get appointments.

At the end of this chapter, there is a clean set of Telechart Cards without my comments.

(DRUM ROLL!)

ONE WORD OF WARNING

Every salesperson that I know would prefer to just wing it. You know, fly right past preparation and just make the phone call and then ad-lib. And, when they finally get a CEO on the phone, they mutter, "Ahh, ahhh, I'd like to speak to Mr. Jones (the CEO)."

"Speaking," the CEO would say.

"Ahhh, ahhh…"

Sorry, too late. That salesperson would have just blown the opportunity to get an appointment with a CEO.

Or sometimes a salesperson winging it would say everything that went through his head in the previous 48 hours:

"Blah, blah, blah, blah, blah……………… blah, blah……. blah,

(More DRUM ROLL!)

Somewhere inside all those blahs, the CEO hung up.

If you want to get the best results with these Telechart Cards, don't ad-lib the cards. Read the cards *word-for-word*. Yep, that's what I said. *Word-for-word*. No embellishing them. No ad-libbing. No adding more language.

WORD-FOR-WORD

Your instincts will tell you to ad-lib. Don't follow your instincts on this. We have trained hundreds of salespeople on the Telechart Cards, and those who stumbled were the ones who didn't follow the cards *exactly*.

Forget about winging it. Go word-for-word-for-word.

Ready?

BRNGGGGGGGGGG... BRNGGGGGGGGGG

SURPRISE #1

You would normally say: 1) Your name; 2) Your company; 3) Your title; 4) Why you're calling. Right? We want you to change the order.

Here's the order we want you to use: 1) Your title; 2) Your team; 3) Your name; 4) Say something that elicits the question, "What is it?" Here's why:

1. **Your title comes first.** When people pick up a ringing phone, they usually aren't too attentive for the first few seconds. Throwing an unknown name (yours) at them will just go unregistered. If you've got a difficult last name like mine, it will fly past the CEO. With our teams, we gave our young salespeople titles that were vague, but sounded important. Note that we didn't use the word *sales* or *tickets*. We used *Corporate Marketing Manager*. A cynic might say that this strategy was sleazy. Not so. I look at a title being a tool to get an appointment. If I could have named all of our young salespeople 'president' I would have, but it didn't seem reasonable that the team would have a 23-year old president. A lot of them.

2. **Your team name second.** By now the CEO is starting to pay attention, a bit. Give the CEO a recognizable name.

CEO: "Hello?"

YOU: "I'm the Corporate Marketing Manager of the Big City Kangaroos and my name is

_____.

(Stage direction. This is just half of your opening. You should read my comments on the left why the information is delivered in this order.)

TELECHART CARD #1

1. **Your name third**. The CEO now has the chance of actually hearing your name. Much more professional than just blurting out your name to an unsuspecting CEO.

2. **Say something that elicits the question, "What is it?"** You have a single reason for calling. That single reason for calling is to get an appointment. That's all. You're not trying to sell tickets over the phone. You need to start a short dialogue that will lead to an appointment. Here's what I say: "I have an idea I think you'd be interested in. It's going to take me 10 minutes to explain. Could we get together for those ten minutes next week?"

Almost every time, the CEO's answer is, "What is the idea?"

> **If you can get the CEO to say "what's the idea" or "what is it?" then you have a terrific chance in getting the appointment.**

Here's what the first Telechart Card looks like: ⇨⇨⇨⇨⇨⇨⇨⇨⇨

YOU: "I have an idea I think you'd be interested in. It's going to take me 10 minutes to explain. Could we get together for those ten minutes next week?

TELECHART CARD #1

YOU: "Hello, I'm the Corporate Marketing Manager of the Big City Kangaroos and my name is _____.
I've got an idea I think you'd be interested in. It's going to take me 10 minutes to explain. Could we get together for those ten minutes next week?

I'm going to be in your area on _____ for a meeting with _____. Can I stop by at _____?"

NOTES ON TELECHART CARD #1

✓ **Succinct**. This is succinct and you're not rambling all over the place. If you ramble, you don't get the appointment.

✓ **The question you want asked.** You're leading the CEO to ask the question, "What is it?" If the CEO asks that question, you have a terrific chance of getting an appointment.

✓ **What you didn't mention.** Note you did not mention tickets at all. Focus on 'an idea' which is purposely vague.

✓ **10 minute timeframe.** Ten minutes is a key theme you'll see throughout all the Telechart Cards. A CEO's life is hectic. If they think you'll take 30-60 minutes, they won't schedule the appointment. For ten minutes, maybe. And, as you'll see in *GETTING THE SALE HANDBOOK*, you can easily give your pitch in 10 minutes.

✓ **Next week.** Ask for the appointment for the following week. CEO's believe the current week is a mess and they optimistically think next week their schedule will be better. A 10-minute meeting *next week* (or the following week) will seem more reasonable.

✓ **In the area.** Mentioning you will be in their area eliminates the CEO giving you the objection of '*I don't want you to waste your time driving out here.*'

✓ **Specific date and time.** Always ask for a specific date and time for a meeting. This forces the CEO to think about his schedule next week for that specific date and time. If you leave it general, it's easier for them to say they are too busy.

(**Stage direction.** You'd think that a simple and easy Opening would not generate this much comment from me. Well, I want you to also *understand* the system. So, read my notes on the left.)

ALTERNATIVE FOR TELECHART CARD #1

NOTES ON TELECHART CARD #1a

For years I used "I've got an idea…" to get appointments with CEOs that ranged from Gillette to General Motors to Miller Beer. In each case, these executives did not know what I was selling. I could've been selling life insurance for all they knew.

When we started using these Telechart Cards with the New Jersey Nets, it was during a recession and the team was really lousy. The salespeople and I felt we needed a statement with a little more bite. Thus, we came up with the statement:

> We've got a *proven* method where you can improve your sales by at least 10% in the next six months. [1]

Everything else was the same. The rest of the Telechart Cards also work for this alternative.

ALTERNATIVE FOR TELECHART CARD #1

CEO: "Hello?"

TELECHART CARD #1a

YOU: "Hello, I'm the Corporate Marketing Manager of the Big City Kangaroos and my name is _____.
We've got a *proven* method where you can improve your sales by at least 10% in the next six months. It's going to take me about ten minutes to explain. Could we get together for those ten minutes next week? I'm going to be in your area next _____ at _____. I can stop by right after that." [1]

---

[1] You'll see in the MAKING THE SALE HANDBOOK that the CEO will definitely be able to increase sales using your tickets.

NOTES ON TELECHART CARD #2

✓ **Succinct**. Again, you're very succinct. You're not saying what the idea is, but you are again asking for 10 minutes.

✓ **The 10 minute timeframe is important.** You've got to convince the CEO that you're only going to take 10 minutes. When pressed, I used to use the following to emphasize the 10 minutes:

> ME: "I'm going to bring in a stopwatch and when I walk through your office door I'm going to click it on and 10 minutes later I'll be walking out your door, unless you ask me to stay for a few more minutes…"

✓ **Specific date and time.** Again, you ask for specifics.

TELECHART CARD #2

CEO: "What is it? What is your idea?"

TELECHART CARD #2

YOU: "It will take me only **10 minutes** to explain—
and I mean only 10 minutes—and if I'm there longer
it's because you asked me to stay. Would
(time)_____ on next (day)_____ be good
for you?"

✓ **Temptation.** You'll be tremendously tempted to tell the CEO *a little* about why you want the appointment. If you try to tell a little, you won't get the appointment.

> Remember, your sole goal for the phone call is to get the appointment. You get the appointment, you achieved this goal.

Hold your ground. The CEO's Gatekeeper (administrative assistant) usually kicks these types of phone calls away. Since you've connected to the CEO directly, and there is no Gatekeeper running interference, most CEOs have only 2-3 rebuttals. So, hold your ground on this one. You're getting closer to an appointment if you don't blow the chance by talking too much.

TELECHART CARD #3

CEO: "I'm really busy. Can you tell me over the phone?"

TELECHART CARD #3

YOU: "I would like to tell you over the phone, but I have something to *show you* and it will just take me 10 minutes and then you can judge for yourself. I want to show you what dozens of other companies are using and are very happy with it—having tremendous success in increasing their sales. I guarantee it will take me just 10 minutes--unless you ask me to stay. How about 10:00am next Tuesday?"

NOTES ON TELECHART CARD #4

You'll find some CEOs very abrupt and discourteously blunt. Those CEOs can easily say they aren't interested without knowing what they aren't interested in. When I get such a response, I sometimes feel like saying, "Well, you oughta be; it's a recession and new revenue dollars are tough to come by."

Instead of saying that, I want to pique the CEOs attention. I say, "That's *precisely* why I called you…" I don't really explain the precisely part, but jump in with a line to put his skepticism with others—others that did see me and benefited by it.

"Many of the people I've talked to weren't interested at first, but after I explained how we could help increase their sales by 10%, they appreciated that we got together."

TELECHART CARD #4

CEO: "I'm not interested."

TELECHART CARD #4

YOU: "That's precisely why I called you, (name of CEO)_____. Many of the people I've talked to weren't interested at first, but after I explained how we could help in increasing their sales by 10%, they appreciated that we got together. I need just 10 minutes, would (time)_____ next (day)_____ be good for you?"

NOTES ON TELECHART CARD #5

Some CEOs are more stubborn than others. That's why you have to be on *ready alert* with your response. As soon as a CEO says 'I'm still not interested' you have to **pounce** on those words almost before the word 'interested' is out of the CEO's mouth. There isn't any delay, you *pounce*. The timeframe between 'interested' and your response is a micro-second.

That's why you need to be prepared, more prepared in making an appointment phone call than anything you could ever imagine.

You might now have a better appreciation of what I wrote earlier:

Never make a cold call on the phone without:

1) knowing what you are going to say;

2) knowing what the prospect will say;

3) knowing how you will respond to the prospect.

As you can see, you have to not only know your material, but you're going to have to use it *under fire and under extreme pressure.*

TELECHART CARD #5

CEO: "I'm still not interested." (2nd time)

TELECHART CARD #5

YOU: "You're probably not interested because what I'm saying sounds so crazy—well, what if it isn't? What if we really can help you increase your sales by 10% over the next six months? It's only going to cost you 10 minutes—and I guarantee that it's only going to be 10 minutes. I'm going to bring a stopwatch and after 10 minutes I'm going to walk out of your office unless you ask me to stay. How about 10:00am next Tuesday?"

NOTES ON TELECHART CARD #6

I'll agree with the CEO on almost anything while trying to make an appointment. For instance, what if he says that I should see the janitor?

CEO: "You should see our janitor…"

ME: "Exactly, I definitely plan on seeing your janitor…"

I don't want to get into a debate with the CEO on which one of his employees I should see. I agree on seeing *any* employee, *after* I meet with the CEO.

LIGHTNING QUICK RESPONSE

Again, you have to be *lightning quick* with your answer. During the sales presentation, there are appropriate times for you to pause; there is no pause in trying to get an appointment.

TELECHART CARD #6

CEO: "You should see our Director of Sales."

TELECHART CARD #6

YOU: "Exactly, I definitely plan to see your Director of Sales at some point. But, I have found that in matters of a proven method of increasing sales by at least 10%, other CEOs really appreciated seeing me first. Could we meet next _____ at _____? I'm meeting with _____ at _____ and can stop by right after."

NOTES ON TELECHART CARD #7

This is a normal objection. If you did send them a proposal in writing, where would it end up? If you said 'trashed' you would be partially correct. The full correct answer would be 'trashed without being opened.'

Many companies are taking this to the electronic level. These companies want you to submit your proposal via a specific website. Now you get 'trashed without a human being even touching it.'

So, I won't debate the CEO's request, and I'll softly agree by saying, 'I can appreciate that,' but I'm not going to elaborate on the fact that putting something in the mail is equivalent to the CEO saying, 'Good-bye.'

TELECHART CARD #7

CEO: "We need to see it in writing first."

TELECHART CARD #7

YOU: "I can appreciate that. Normally I'd be happy to, but I have something I need to show you. I want to show you what a number of other executives have been using. It's only going to take 10 minutes and you can judge for yourself. Could we meet next Tuesday at 10:00am?"

NOTES ON TELECHART CARD #8

Again, I don't debate it. So, what if the CEO isn't a fan of a particular sport or of any sport for that matter?

TELECHART CARD #8

CEO: "I'm not a baseball fan.*"

TELECHART CARD #8

YOU: "I can understand that, but I have an idea that would center on profit, not baseball.

You don't have to be a baseball fan to like this.

Could we meet next Tuesday at 10:00am?"

* **Stage Direction.** The CEO translated your team's nickname to a particular sport, in this example, baseball. It could be basketball, football, hockey, whatever. Your response would be the same.

What we're doing is much more that schlepping a bunch of tickets.

We're selling a *system* that the CEO can have utilized to help increase that company's revenue. It would be very difficult to explain over the phone—that's what we need the 10-minute meeting for. So, our answer here might be considered a bit of misdirection saying that 'It *could* include tickets,' but it doesn't have to be tickets. Once you're with the CEO it might become very apparent that the CEO needs a *sponsorship—not tickets*—and you can arrange a meeting with the CEO and one of your sponsorship executives.

TELECHART CARD #9

CEO: "Is this about tickets?"

TELECHART CARD #9

YOU: "It could include tickets, but it's more about *increasing profits*. This has been successful for other CEOs—in fact do you know...(name of company & CEO) _____?

He loved this idea and is implementing it right now.

Could I make an appointment for next _____at_____?"

NOTES ON TELECHART CARD #10

Many executives get in early and many stay late and many come in on Saturday mornings. These CEOs often *appreciate* a young salesperson that is willing and enthusiastic about meeting early in the morning or late in the day or on a Saturday. In fact, most CEOs wish that their company had a salesperson who was that socially-acceptably aggressive.

We had a young salesperson with the New Jersey Nets that was talking to a CEO of a produce company. The exec's answer to the start of his day was, "4:00am."

Our young salesperson gulped and said, "I'll be on your doorstep at 4:00am next Tuesday, before you really get started. I'll even bring the coffee. Do you prefer black coffee or cream and sugar?"

Sure, the young salesperson made the sale. The CEO almost feels *obligated* to buy when a salesperson shows that type of initiative. The young salesperson also got a job offer from that CEO, but our young salesperson was having too much fun selling our stuff.

TELECHART CARD #10

CEO: "Look, I don't really have the time."

TELECHART CARD #10

YOU: "What time do you start your day?"

(The CEO responds with 7:00am)*

"I'll be on your doorstep at 7:00am next Tuesday, before you really get started. I'll even bring the coffee. Do you prefer black coffee or cream and sugar?

I'll be there no longer than 10 minutes unless you ask me to stay long enough to finish my coffee."

(* You're fishing here. If the CEO doesn't come in early, you ask how late do they stay or ask if they work on Saturday mornings. You're trying to find a time that doesn't normally fit an average day.)

NOTES ON TELECHART CARD #11

This is the *third pass* at the CEO saying that he isn't interested. Rarely does it come down to that, but you have to be ready. You can't just reiterate what you said before.

With this card, you get to do a little name dropping. The name you give here doesn't have to be a well-known executive or even a well-known company. Just the name dropping adds a little credibility and allows you to again say how you value the CEO's time.

TELECHART CARD #11

CEO: "I don't think I'm interested."

TELECHART CARD #11

YOU: "Well, (name of an exec who bought)_____
of (company name)_____ wasn't interested
either, but after we met he liked some of the truly
unique ideas that we discussed. I value your time and I
wouldn't be in your office more than 10 minutes. My
feeling is that you would appreciate that we did get
together. Could we meet next Tuesday at 10:00am?"

NOTES ON TELECHART CARD #12

What are your chances of connecting with the CEO the following week? None. It's not a small chance, it's no chance. The CEO just wants to get off the phone with you right now.

Since my chances are zero in re-connecting, I'm going to give it another shot and just ask for a specific time slot.

If necessary, I might offer to confirm the appointment. I would say something like this: "I'll call the day before to make sure that time is still solid."

I rarely do call to confirm. I usually just show up for the designated time. Sometimes there are no problems. Sometimes the CEO's administrative assistant comes out to the lobby and says that I was supposed to call to confirm. I am *very apologetic* saying that when I called on my cell phone I was out of range, etc., etc.

I then ask to set up another time, which I usually get with the caveat that I call to confirm. This time I do indeed call.

TELECHART CARD #12

CEO: "Call me next week and I'll see what my schedule looks like."

TELECHART CARD #12

YOU: "I have my schedule handy, is yours handy? Why don't we just set a time right now? Is 10:00am next Tuesday good for you?"

NOTES ON TELECHART CARD #13

As you can see, I don't try to debate the point or talk about all the improvements we expect for next season. I say, "I *understand…*" and then I swing into how even 'under current conditions we can help.'

WILD CARD TELECHART CARD #13

CEO: "Your team is lousy."

TELECHART CARD #13

YOU: "I can understand how you feel. We haven't been as good as we would like. That will change. But, what I want to meet with you about is that even under current conditions we have a unique idea how we can help increase your sales by 10% over a six month period. How about 10:00am next Tuesday?"

CONFIRMATION!

CEO: "Okay, next Tuesday at 8:00am"

YOU: "Terrific, you're really going to like what I have to show you.

I've got you down in my book for next Tuesday at 8:00am.

Is that what you have in yours?"

YOU: "Can I get your email address to send you a confirmation?"

WHO DICTATES YOUR SUCCESS?

A personal note from Jon Spoelstra

In the second year I was the president of the New Jersey Nets, we were developing some real sharpshooters in ticket sales. Some of these guys were getting appointments like it was *easy*. Well, they made it easy because of their work ethic.

This changed a bit when we had a rookie sales guy come in. In the first month he led the ticket sales staff in sales! That not only surprised me; it surprised those sharpshooters on the staff too.

Then in the second month the rookie does it again. He led the sales staff in sales. He was proving it wasn't a fluke.

Then, sure enough, he led the sales staff again in sales for the third straight month.

This rookie didn't look the part of a salesperson that had led this staff for three straight months. His best clothes were from Sears. He drove a dumpy pick-up truck. But he beat a staff—a staff full of sharpshooters—in sales for three straight months.

Then the next month he was eighth in sales.

The month after that he was 10th out of 20 salespeople.

His monthly ranking looked like this: 1,1,1,8,10.

Something was wrong.

One day after work, I took him out for a beer.

I said, "You led this sales staff for three straight months, you're the first one in the office, you're the last one to leave, and now you rank in the middle of the pack, and you drag in to work and you leave early. What's up?"

I suspected drugs.

He denied anything was wrong.

We had a couple more beers.

He finally said, "I want to be liked."

"Huh?" I said.

"When I was leading the sales staff," he said, "nobody was very friendly to me. I'm new to the area and didn't know anybody, and nobody on the sales staff included me for beers or even conversations. So, I decided to be more *accessible*. I decided that I wanted to be liked by the rest of the staff, and when I was leading in sales, I don't think they liked me. Now they're starting to warm up a bit."

"Bull," I said.

"Huh?" he said.

"So, you're going to let your acquaintances choose what type of life you're going to live?" I said.

"I don't think so," he said.

"Well, you've done it here," I said. "You let guys you hardly know dictate—and they didn't even know they were dictating—how successful you would be. Maybe they'd warm up even more if you were ranked 19th or dead last at 20th. But, then I'd probably fire you. Look, these guys that are on this staff are terrific guys. They came in with no experience just like you. I think the only thing they would respect is for you to *compete* with them. I'd rather make friends on *my* terms than on other's perceived terms, which would be mediocrity."

"I hadn't thought of it that way," he said.

"We aren't training our salespeople to be mediocre. We're training our salespeople to be tremendous successes in life. It starts with you getting back on that leaderboard."

He did. He was tremendously successful after the Nets, and is a leader in our industry today. His success happened when he *decided to dictate to his own success*.

WOULD YOU DO IT?

Let's say for the moment that you play golf. Your handicap is 15. That basically means that you're 15 strokes over par.

Let's also say that I could provide Tiger Woods' former coach, Hank Haney, to be your personal coach. There would be no cost to you. As your personal coach, Haney would work with you for an hour a day for three months. At the end of that time, your handicap would be reduced to 0. That would put you in the top 1% of all golfers. You'd be close to what the pros on tour shoot.

Before I flew Hank Haney in, I would ask you one question:

Would you do it?

It's only an hour a day for three months.

But during that hour, Haney would probably change everything you know about golf.

He'd change your grip. He'd change your takeaway. He'd change your swing. He'd change *everything*! But, at the end of three months you'd be a scratch golfer.

Would you do it?

Some would say *yes*, but then falter along the way. They'd stop going to the lessons every day. Others would say *no* because golf wasn't that important to them. They were satisfied with a 15 handicap. A select few would say *yes* and get Hank's lessons every day for three months and become a scratch golfer.

Now, let's look at your career.

Let's say you *can* become a *great* ticket salesperson. Let's say that the skills you learned here would give you an advantage for the rest of your life. You would be more successful than you could have ever dreamed. But, to achieve that success you would have to spend one hour a day for three months on perfecting the sales fundamentals. One hour a day, seven days a week, for three months.

Would you do it?

The fundamentals we have brought to you in the MAKING THE APPOINTMENT HANDBOOK and MAKING THE SALE HANDBOOK need to be practiced. It's like hitting a golf ball every day under Hank Haney's tutelage. Sure, you would dramatically improve. Well, here you would be practicing making the appointment and making the sale under my tutelage. I, of course, won't physically be by your side, but my philosophies are here at your fingertips. What is needed is *your practice*. An hour a day for three months.

If you did indeed practice an hour a day for three months, you would have a spectacular advantage. Would you do it? Some would say *yes*, but then falter along the way. They'd stop taking that hour a day to practice. They were getting 'good enough.' Being *great* wasn't that important to them. Others would say *no* because ticket sales wasn't that important to them. They were satisfied on just being in the sports industry.

A very select few would say *yes* and practice the fundamentals in both of my handbooks every day for three months and become great at ticket sales. Those select few just put themselves on a different rung of the career ladder, a ladder that will lead to spectacular things.

Would you do it?

TELECHART CARDS

The following four pages are our sample Telechart Cards for your use.
Here's my recommendation on how to use them:

1. Type the cards onto cover stock the size of about 3.5" x 8"
2. One Telechart Card per each 3.5" x 8" card.
3. Personalize the cards with your team name and your name.
4. Don't just become familiar with them. Learn them, memorize them, *feel* them.
5. Add additional cards for any new objections you receive on a semi-regular basis.

I'm the corporate marketing manager of the (team) _____. My name is _____. **I've got an idea that I think you would be interested in.** It's going to take me 10 minutes to explain. Could we get together for those ten minutes next week? I'm going to be in your area on _____ for a meeting with _____ I can stop by at _____?

Answer: What is it?

© Jon Spoelstra

Answer: It will take me only **10 minutes** to explain—and I mean only 10 minutes—and if I'm there longer it's because you asked me to stay. Would _____ on _____ be good for you or would _____ be better?

© Jon Spoelstra

We've got a *proven* method where you can improve your sales by at least 10% in the next six months. It's going to take me about ten minutes to explain. Could we get together for those ten minutes next week?

I'm going to be in your area next _____ at _____. I can stop by right after that.

© Jon Spoelstra

Answer: I would like to tell you over the phone, but I have something to show you and it will just take me 10 minutes and then you can judge for yourself. I want to show you what dozens of other companies are using and are very happy with it--having tremendous success in increasing their sales. I guarantee it will take me just 10 minutes--unless you ask me to stay. How about 10:00am next Tuesday?

© Jon Spoelstra

66

Another objection "I'm not interested."	**Even another objection** "I'm not interested." (2nd time)	**Another objection** "You should see our Director of Sales."	**And another objection** "We need to see it in writing first."

Answer: That's precisely why I called you, _____. Many of the people that I've talked to weren't interested at first, but after I explained how we could help in increasing their sales by 10%, they appreciated that we got together. I need just 10 minutes, would _____ at _____ be good for you?

You're probably not interested because what I'm saying sounds so crazy—well, what if it isn't? What if we really can help you increase your sales by 10% over the next six months. It's only going to cost you 10 minutes—and I guarantee that it's only going to be 10 minutes. I'm going to bring a stop watch and after 10 minutes I'm going to walk out of your office unless you ask me to stay.
How about 10:00am next Tuesday?

Answer: Exactly, I definitely plan to see your Director of Sales at some point. But, I have found that in matters of a proven method of increasing sales by at least 10% that other CEOs really appreciated seeing me first. Could we meet next _____ at _____? I'm meeting with _____ at _____ and can stop by right after.

Answer: I can appreciate that. Normally I'd be happy to but I have something I need to show you. I want to show you what a number of other executives have been using. It's only going to take 10 minutes and you can judge for yourself. Could we meet next Tuesday at 10:00am?

Another objection
"I'm not a baseball fan."

Answer: I can understand that, but I have an idea that would centers on profits, not baseball. You don't have to be a baseball fan to like this. Could we meet next Tuesday at 10:00am?

Another objection
"I don't think I'm interested."

Answer: Well, M._____ of _____ wasn't interested either, but after we met he liked some of the truly unique ideas that we discussed. I value your time and I wouldn't be in your office more than 10 minutes. My feeling is that you would appreciate that we did get together. Could we meet next Tuesday at 10:00am?

One last objection
"Is this about tickets?"

Answer: It could include tickets, but it's more about *increasing profits*. This has been successful for other CEOs—in fact do you know... (name of company & CEO) _____? He loved this idea and is implementing it right now. Could I make an appointment for next _____ at_____?

Last gasp objection
"Look, I really don't have the time"

YOU: What time do you start your day?

(He responds with 7:00am)

I'll be on your doorstep at 7:00am next Tuesday, before you really get started. I'll even bring the coffee. Do you prefer black coffee or cream and sugar?

Confirmation

"Terrific, you're really going to like what I have to show you.

I've got you down in my book for next _____ at _____

Is that what you have in yours?"

69

Made in the USA
Lexington, KY
30 January 2018